THE COMPLETE BOOK OF FARTING

*And suddenly there came a sound
from heaven
as of a rushing mighty wind, and
it filled all the house where they
were sitting.*

THE ACTS OF THE APOSTLES 2:2

THE COMPLETE BOOK OF FARTING

BY ALEC BROMCIE

MICHAEL O'MARA BOOKS LIMITED

First published in Great Britain in 1999 by
Michael O'Mara Books Limited
9 Lion Yard
Tremadoc Road
London SW4 7NQ

A CIP catalogue record for this book is available from the British Library

ISBN 1-85479-440-X

1 3 5 7 9 10 8 6 4 2

Original concept and compilation by David Crombie
Designed and typeset by DESIGN 23
Printed and bound by Cox & Wyman

ABOUT THE AUTHOR

Alec Bromcie is Visiting Professor of Wind and Sound at the University of Valparaiso. He is the author of many academic papers and theses on the subject of farting and has decided to publish his latest ideas and research findings in this book.

Among his recent accomplishments is his research into farting at high altitude, which won him the prestigious Yak Award from the University of Nepal.

At present he is working on the development of a 'fartometer' – an appliance that can detect the source of a fart. Inspired by the biblical quote 'The wind bloweth where it listeth, and thou hearest the sound thereof, but canst not tell whence it cometh, and whither it goeth' (John 3:8), Professor Bromcie has made it his ambition to put an end to those 'Who's farted?' conversations. He claims that his fartometer will, within a second of the emission, be able to pinpoint the perpetrator.

He is currently single, has three children, two pet skunks and lives in Pratts Bottom, England.

He can be contacted at
alec.bromcie@michaelomarabooks.com

PUBLISHER'S DISCLAIMER

Any person who attempts either of the following does so at their own risk: lighting farts or trying out Mother Bromcie's farting recipes. The first practice is deemed by both the publisher and the author to be a dangerous and infantile pastime, and although there are passing references to it in the book, at no stage is it advocated. It should be noted that the publisher has neither tried nor tested Mother Bromcie's recipes, and therefore recommends that participants proceed with extreme caution and that they should reduce some of the ingredients such as curry powder.

While the statistics in this book have been verified by the publisher wherever possible, all statistical information was provided by the author. All names in Dr Bromcie's case studies have been changed to protect the identity and preserve the modesty of the individuals involved.

CONTENTS

ACKNOWLEDGEMENTS

I would like to thank all those who have contributed to this book.

An especially big trumpet to my fellow colleague and partner in crime, Yvette, who gave me insight into the female side of farting. Also, to my esteemed mother, Mrs Bromcie; where would I be without her sprout curry?

A big toot to my publisher Michael O'Mara who was sufficiently blown away by the contents of this book to agree to publish it.

Smaller but sweeter heralds to my wonderful team of researchers and statisticians: Jacquie Wind, Helen Blowers, Toby Bucksnort, Emma Breezer and Alex BelAir. At times their enthusiasm for this subject worried me slightly.

Last, but by no means least, to my faithful fan club. I would ask you to keep sending me your true stories of farting experiences – who knows, they may well appear in my next book.

A LITTLE BIT OF PARPING ON TO BEGIN WITH

THE DINOSAURS

I have often wondered why the dinosaurs became extinct. But it really isn't that hard, is it? All that gas they produced must have gradually poisoned them – I mean, can you imagine the blast that occurred when a brontosaurus lifted its tail? Brontosorearse more like. The addition of extra methane and hydrogen sulphide to the atmosphere polluted the prevailing eco-system and one by one they keeled over.

THE CAVE MEN

Early man was, as we now know, a carnivore, although before that all those berries, nuts and roots for which he foraged must have provided him with enough essential ingredients – for farting, that is. We can only imagine what the atmosphere was like in the caves when they returned, full-bellied, from hunting. All that adrenaline would have got the old metabolism really activated – I mean, how would you feel if you were pitting your flint against a mammoth or a sabre-tooth tiger? As they relaxed back in their caves, their women must have been really pleased to see them. It is my theory that the reason why in some cultures women eat in a different room to their men, or leave the table as soon as they've wolfed dessert, is a throwback to the cavemen. Can you blame them? (Of course, the myth that women never fart has recently been exploded, as I will detail in this book.)

THE ROMANS

It was the Romans who got farting properly sussed. All those eight-course dinners and lying down while they ate did thunders for the digestion. Hadrian's Wall was quite probably a crude attempt by the Scots to keep the Roman farts in as opposed to a Roman endeavour to keep the Scots out.

THE ELIZABETHANS

The Elizabethans got a bit more practical about farting. With their huge skirts and puffy breeches, a bit of wind actually helped to raise them to the height of fashion. Meanwhile, their ruffs could act as fans to stop unpleasant odours wafting upwards, and of course they carried bags of spices so that even the most noisome farts could be sweetened somewhat.

This idea was still in evidence in the Victorian era, but the habit of lacing people up to make them look thinner hampered the digestion somewhat. Stays were designed to keep the ribcage in, and consequently, the air out, so we can conclude that in the nineteenth century they were a farty lot of folk.

FARTING TODAY

And farting today? Well that's where I come in and is largely the purpose of this book. I have spent years researching farting, and in *The Complete Book of Farting* I have tried to bring together all the details I think will be of interest to general readers. While the book is based on scientific fact, proven statistics and my own case studies, my intention is not only to inform but to amuse. Some readers will be surprised at how unstuffy this book may seem when compared to my regular theses, but most will delight in this fresh and breezy approach. Critics should remember that I am always happy to have my work referred to as a lot of old wind.

I dedicate this book to all those who fart – and those that don't (admit it!).

Bottoms up!

ALEC BROMCIE, PRATTS BOTTOM 1999

12

A GENERAL INTRODUCTION TO FARTING

Let's get this straight to begin with – everybody farts. FARTS ARE 100 PER CENT NORMAL! They are a vital and inescapable part of everyday life and are nothing to be prudish about. When God created man, and notably woman, he meant them to do what comes naturally, and fart away Adam and Eve no doubt did, particularly with all those fruit trees around.

The Old Testament aside, flatulence has an ancient and honourable history, at least where the medical profession is concerned. The great Hippocrates of Cos (*c*. 460 BC – *c*. 377, *c*. 359 or *c*. 357 BC; the authorities differ) made certain that doctors should understand the mechanics of farting, and they and their patients the consequences. If some of his theories have not withstood the test of time and the relentless march of medicine – hardly very surprising, given that he was practising some 2,300 years ago – he remains sound on flatulence. Of the consequences of farting, he had this to say of the avoidance of what patent-medicine advertisements call 'abdominal pain':

It is best to pass wind noiselessly, but even a noisy fart is better than one retained . . . Pains and swelling in the *hypochondria* [situated in the upper abdomen, and believed by the ancient Greeks to be the seat of melancholy] are much reduced by *borborygmi* [rumblings of gas in the intestines] in the *hypochondrium* [upper abdomen] . . . much relief will be effected by the gas moving along, and also by its descent to the lower bowels.

Hippocrates seems, too, to have had a pretty good sense not only of the nature of farting, but also of how the human body operates:

The factors that cause flatulence or *tormina* ['acute griping or ringing pains in the bowels' – *OED*; the word derives from the same root as 'torment'] . . . naturally do so in the hollow parts of the body, the stomach and chest, where they produce rumbling noises . . .

Among other things – for which, read on –

I came like Water and like Wind I go
EDWARD FITZGERALD, *THE RUBÁIYÁT OF OMAR KHAYYÁM*

WHAT IS A FART?

Farts are nature's way of releasing our own toxins. Flatulence can be described as the pressure of excessive amounts of gas in the stomach or intestines. If we didn't fart, the gases we produce would be reabsorbed into the blood and poison us. And, as anyone who has ever suffered from trapped wind can verify, holding it in causes painful swelling and distension of the abdomen. In the many years I have devoted to the subject of farting, I haven't heard of a single human being who has actually filled to bursting point – unlike cows which explode regularly.

Farts are mainly composed of five gases:

Nitrogen (N_2)
Carbon dioxide (CO_2)
Hydrogen (H_2)
Methane (CH_4)
Oxygen (O_2)

WHAT'S IN A FART?

The gases listed above are OK so far as it goes, but hydrogen, nitrogen and oxygen are elements and by themselves will not got give the true flavour of a fart. What they need is a bit of spicing up and they get this by forming compounds with carbon (C) and sulphur (S). Thus, the method of creation of such essential smell-factor ingredients as skatol (C_9H_9N) which is composed of nine parts carbon, nine parts hydrogen and one part nitrogen.

Of course, each and every fart will vary, but there have to be some standards – we're talking science here, not social. To get to the fart of the matter, if you'll forgive the pun, I have listed the properties of the various components of a fart below:

Properties of Carbon Dioxide (or Carbon-acid gas):
- A heavy gas which accounts for up to 50-60% of the gas in a fart
- Formed during respiration and the combustion of organic compounds
- Dissolves in water to make carbonic acid, H_2CO_3, which is what makes drinks fizzy and, in turn, what results in those bubbles in the bath
- Does not support combustion hence is used in fire-

extinguishers (worth noting for those that must set light to their farts!)

- Also colourless so it won't be responsible for those unfortunate brown marks that can sometimes appear on men's underpants (no woman has ever admitted to this happening to her).
- CO_2 is heavier than air so that its presence in a smelly fart also means that the smell tends to hang around. (NB. CO_2 is absorbed by plants through photosynthesis, so if you get caught out fart under a tree.)
- CO_2 is a suffocating gas but not toxic — unlike carbon monoxide which might finish you off if you farted in a cupboard for a few days
- Can be narcotic in high quantities (i.e. CO_2 narcosis)

Properties of Nitrogen:
- Predominates in farting by the formation of compounds such as indol and skatol
- Colourless
- Odourless
- Relatively unreactive
- Forms 78% of the air we breathe

Properties of Hydrogen
- The lightest and most abundant element in the universe
- Highly flammable

- Stinks when reacted with sulphur to form the compound hydrogen sulphide
- Colourless
- Used in the formation of bombs in which energy is released by fusion of hydrogen nuclei

Properties of Methane
- Also known as natural gas or marsh gas. Methane is produced by the decomposition of organic matter, and swamps, marshes and river-beds often contain large amounts of decomposing vegetation. Since the food we eat also undergoes a process of decomposition (due to the action of *E. coli* microbes in the large bowel), and since food is almost entirely organic matter, it is not at all surprising that methane is present in farts
- Flammable: when lit will appear as a strong blue or green flame – DON'T TRY IT!
- Increased by eating beans
- Makes coal mines explode. Methane is a product of the carbonization of coal. The explosive mixture of hydrocarbons, mainly methane, found in coal mines is known as 'firedamp'; after a firedamp explosion a poisonous mixture of gases, mostly our old friend carbon monoxide, is left; this is known as 'afterdamp', while the mixture of poisonous gases just generally found in mines – chiefly carbon monoxide – is called 'whitedamp'. It is a

little known fact that miners never fart – they have enough to worry about without adding 'browndamp' to their problems.

- Methane from the flatulence of cattle and sheep is said to be damaging the ozone layer.
- Tarzan, who lived entirely on jungly vegetables, was greeted by his lady friend with the wrinkled-nose exclamation: 'You! Tarzan – Methane!'

Properties of Oxygen:
- Colourless, tasteless, odourless, highly reactive; essential for all aerobic respiration and almost all combustion
- Commonest element in the Earth's crust
- There are often only low levels of this gas in a fart but recycling it is essential for human life
- Found in the compound CO_2 (see above)

Methyl-indol (US: methyl-indole):
- Methyl, CH_3, is derived from methane by the removal of one hydrogen atom
- Indol, C_8H_7N, is a crystalline compound derived from decomposing proteins (i.e. grub)
- Amazingly, since its smell would curl flock wallpaper in a curry house at 100 paces, it is used in making scent

Skatol (US: skatole) – C_9H_9N

- The name, charmingly, derives from Greek *skor, skatos*, dung, from which we also derive words like scatological
- Foul-smelling
- Also in civet; hence it, too, is used in scent-making

Hydrogen Sulphide (rotten-egg gas) – H_2S
- Colourless
- Inflammable
- Soluble in water
- Poisonous
- This one's a real stinker . . .

Methyl-mercaptan
- For the methyl bit see above under Methyl-indol
- Mercaptan is any of various compounds that contain a thiol, the latter being one of several compounds analogous with alcohols but where sulphur replaces the oxygen of the hydroxyl group

Enough, I think, of science lesson number one, although for serious students I am always happy to provide further details of what goes on in the chemical laboratory of our bottoms.

On to science lesson number two:

HOW DO WE FART?

The causes of tympanites are aerophagy, acute dilation of the stomach, mechanical intestinal obstruction and paralytic ileus.

(THESIS ON FARTING NO. 2345 A. BROMCIE)

Let's start at that very good place to begin – the beginning. Every time we open our mouths or breathe through our noses we are starting off an extraordinary chain of events. We take in air and, as we all know, what goes in must come out – about 8 metres of digestive tract later. A fart begins by swallowing air. It then travels down into the stomach where, at this stage, it will be mainly composed of atmospheric nitrogen and oxygen – i.e. not much yet has happened to it. If all is going well and our insides are in regular working order, some of the oxygen will be absorbed here. However, nitrogen is largely unabsorbable and so merrily meanders on through our intestines.

It is in the intestines that carbon dioxide, methane and hydrogen are formed. The carbon dioxide, produced by fermentation, is largely absorbed.

It is a fact of life that man (or woman) cannot fart on air alone. To make a decent fart, a loud, noisy, juicy or smelly one, he (she) needs some protein and some carbo-hydrate – i.e. some grub. During the digestion of food and the sorting out of the leftovers, bacteria ferment away, attacking the remains of our latest snack and blasting the food that has not been fully digested in the small or large intestine. It is at this stage that the other gases we have mentioned are produced. What we eat is important to the volume and composition of farts. Some foods prove harder to digest than others – i.e. foods which are rich in starch or cellulose such as cabbage (see Food For Farters) – and these are the ones that farters love. The much maligned baked bean, for example, is a complex carbohydrate that is just mal-digested. And the same holds true for mushrooms. Many people don't realize that mushrooms contain a sugar called raffinose, which humans can't break down. The outcome: GAS!

Now we are getting ready for it. We are on amber light. The gases are all mixing together nicely, the sphincter muscle is on standby and the gases – now called flatus – are coming down the rectum. Check that the situation is a green light one and that it's suitable to pull away and PARP! – you have a fart.

Note: Gas, of course, is not the only result of Voidance. So for those that would prefer Avoidance of certain nasty accidents - do be careful where and when you let go.

HOW OFTEN DO WE FART?

The *Guinness Book Of Records* holds statistics on neither the longest, the loudest, nor the smelliest fart, or the most in one day, month or year. In fact, surprisingly, it holds no statistics on the subject whatsoever. Never fear! From my own research into the subject of farting and through my attendance at the many farting conferences that are held each year throughout the world, I have come to the following reliable conclusions:

• Most of us pass somewhere between 200 and 2,000 ml of gas each and every day (that's an average of about 600 ml). An interesting thought for the next time that you breathe in a gulp of 'fresh' air.

• In one study I performed the results were that on average we pass wind 10–20 times a day, and in a study of men of about 20-40 years of age with healthily functioning bowels, the average number of gas eruptions was 16 times a day.

I have come across one study which makes a case for a man living in Oklahoma who farted as often as 145 times daily, including 83 farts in one four-hour period. I have yet to come across this human hurricane, but I would dearly love to meet him or anyone else that can make such an impressive claim.

There is a cheat's method to farting and that is to suck back in the air after letting go a fart and then to release it again. In this way one draws air back into the colon and can fart and fart, and fart again.

Vital statistics:
It is possible to go a whole day without farting but in general my vital statistics are:

Average volume of passage of wind in healthy male:
- 600 ml.

Average number of passages:
- Man: 15–17 farts in 24 hours
- Woman: 8–9 farts in 24 hours
    (OK they do it less but they do do it!)

Record statistics:
- 2,000 ml
- 145 farts in 24 hours
- 70 farts in 4 hours

DID YOU KNOW?
• The average man releases enough flatus in a day to blow up a small balloon
• The war of farting between the sexes is equal on all matters of sound and smell

WHY ARE SOME FARTS NOISY AND SOME NOT?

Why are some farts honest and loud and others silent and deadly? Well here is one theory:

Vegetarians

Vegetarianism is harmless enough, though it is apt to fill a man with wind and self-righteousness
                                    SIR ROBERT HUTCHINSON

Vegetarians fart more often than meat-eaters because their diet is harder to digest. They also fart more quietly as all that roughage loosens the sphincter muscles. Just for the record, the farts do tend to be particularly offensive to the nostrils. For those who would like to have quiet farts, without turning veggie, let that air out very slowly and you might just get away with it.

Carnivores

Carnivores fart less than their veggie friends but, since they have tighter sphincters and go to the loo less often due to lack of roughage, they build up more pressure and hence are the greater reverberators. Squeezing the buttocks together may let out a fart bit by bit, but it can also result in a roaring blast. Be careful if you find yourself trying this in a lift or on a train at rush-hour.

WHY DO FARTS SMELL?

The disagreeable odour of flatus is caused by several sulphur compounds, particularly by mercaptans, (which are too complicated to explain here).

Everyone has a different mixture of gases causing different smells. Also, some farts will contain greater amounts of heavy gas so that they will hang around longer than others.

DID YOU KNOW?
Like all good perfumes, after two minutes farts becomes odourless to our noses.

DID YOU KNOW?
If you fart into a bottle and put the cork back in, or into

an airtight tin, you can preserve your ripest farts for some time – although I deem it very anti-social to do this in someone else's flask or lunchbox.

WHAT IS THE LONGEST FART?

The time a fart hangs around depends on what foods one has eaten and how much gas was expelled. Farts can travel as far as 15 metres and the smell can linger for two to five minutes, although I have also recorded twenty minutes.

HOT FARTS

The heat of the moment can be very embarrassing – yes we all know the danger of hot farts! To understand why some farts are ringburners we need to go back to our internal chemistry lab. Basically, if you have a very full intestine, the particles inside rush round more quickly than usual and in the process produce heat which hots up our gas. Some foods such as curry and chili also affect the heat in our intestines – hence the power of the good old curry fart.

The intestines are the home of tempests: in them is formed gas, as in the clouds

BRILLAT-SAVARIN

ARE BURPS THE SAME AS FARTS?

The exit of gas by mouth (eructation) or by anus (fart)

MEDICAL DEFINITION

Are burps the same as farts? Nope! Repeated belching indicates aerophagia. Some persons with this problem can readily produce a series of belches on command. This form of belching is due to unconscious, repeated aspiration of air into the aesophagus, often in response to stress, followed by rapid expulsion.

CAN YOU EVER SEE A FART?

In a word, no. (Unless you set light to one which doesn't strictly speaking count.)

Let us now move on to the essential subject of food: specifically, of course, foods which makes you fart . . .

FOOD FOR FARTERS

Pardon me for being rude
It was not me, it was my food . . .

One is always being told by Establishment figures to watch what one eats. Likewise, I tell all my students to eat a rich and varied diet and to record the effects on their digestive systems. As it goes, the diet is even quite healthy, with most students finding their research easier if they eat plenty of roughage, fruit and vegetables. Beer and carbonated drinks might pile on the calories but they also help pile on the farts, so my students feel they are a necessary 'evil'. As you enter my laboratory you will see a large sign on the wall which says:

'Are you getting your daily fart intake?
Do you fart what you eat?'

Below is a list of foods that make you fart. You may like to make your own fart chart, recording size, noise, length of fart and pungency. Certainly, compare notes against mine.

Food	Notable Properties 1-10	Fart rating on scale of 1-10	Personal Log 1-10
APRICOTS	Renowned (historically) for giving sailors the runs	2	
BAKED BEANS:	59 varieties to play havoc with our digestive system	10	
BEER	Austrian or German variety recommended	10	
BRAN	Good for those that want to start the day on the right note	5	
BRUSSELS SPROUTS	Real Christmas crackers	10	
CABBAGE	Watered-down version of the sprout	7	

CHEWING GUM	Indigestible and encourages the swallowing of air	3
CHILLI	Hot Stuff!	10
CURRY	Sometimes even Hotter Stuff!	10
EGGS	Contain sulphur so great for stinky farts	10
FIGS	Rather exotic	5
GARLIC	Good for the heart	5
LEEKS	Long, strong and healthy	9
LENTILS	Side-splitting	8
MILK	Good for people with sensitivity to dairy products	4

NUTS	Varies according to type	4
ONION	Some good peals from this one	10
PEAS	Small but deadly — careful of mushy variety	8
PICKLES	Spicy ones make the best farts	8
PLUMS	Squelchy, fart with care	8
PRUNES:	As plums	8

RASPBERRIES The farting expression 'raspberry' is rhyming slang for 'raspberry tart'. However, most people who have taken part in my studies have not found this particular berry troublesome. Hence

| | it is sensible to conclude that the number of raspberries used in the tart must determine the effect on the eater | 4 |

| SPICES | Good for irritating the gut, and for the final flavour | 7 |

| SCOTCH EGGS | No wonder the Scots wear kilts! | 10 |

| STEAK | Hearty, loud and beefy | 8 |

| TRIPE | Not too meaty | 6 |

| WATERCRESS | Strictly vegetarian | 5 |

MOTHER BROMCIE'S FARTING RECIPES

For those who WANT to increase their fart ratings I recommend the diet I feed to all my laboratory animals. Indeed I myself, my dear mother Mrs Bromcie and my laboratory assistants partake of these dishes frequently during our studies. Obviously my digestive system is attuned to this sort of diet, but my publisher has asked me to state that anyone trying these recipes at home does so entirely at their own risk and that the publisher cannot be responsible for any 'anti-social consequences'.

So, over to the kitchen and Mother Bromcie.

My fulsome and nutritious recipes have been handed down through generations of Bromcie cooks, each of whom has added his or her unique variations to the original dish. An evil rumour has been circulating amongst the culinary masters of Europe and the United States that my celebrated meals cannot be achieved without specialist equipment and unusual ingredients. These calumnies are the product of envy – it is perfectly possible to produce splendid results with the contents of a well-stocked store cupboard and ordinary kitchen utensils.

You will need:
A blender, food processor or hand whisk
Sharp knife
Large bowl
A medium-sized saucepan
An omelette pan
A deep–fat fryer

Store cupboard ingredients

Garlic powder	Curry powder
Chilli powder	Canned baked beans
Dried chillies	Dried apricots
Eggs	Canned beer
White bread	Spam

SPROUT CURRY

I find this healthy and startling curry is just the thing to tempt young men, (who can often be particular and fussy eaters when it comes to green vegetables) especially following the success of their chosen football or Rugby football club team.

1.5 kilos fresh, green Brussels sprouts
  (washed and outer leaves removed)
250 fl oz water
$^1/_2$ x 5 ml spoon salt
25 g butter
1 onion, peeled and finely chopped
$2^1/_2$ x 5 ml curry powder
$^1/_2$ x 5 ml ground coriander
$^1/_4$ x 5 ml ground ginger

1. Using a sharp knife, make a small cross in the base of each sprout and place in a large saucepan. Cover with cold, salted water. Leave to soak for 30 minutes. Drain and place in 250 fl oz cold water and $1/2$ teaspoon of salt. Bring to the boil, then simmer for 15 minutes or until soft. Drain, and mash to a pulp using a potato masher.

2. Meanwhile, melt the butter in a large frying pan. Add the onion and cook until transparent but not brown.

3. Add the sprout pulp to the frying pan and stir over a low heat until the sprouts are heated through.

4. Stir in the curry powder, ground coriander and ginger, and cook for a further 15 minutes.

5. Serve piping hot as an accompaniment to Deep-Fried Scotch Eggs (page 39) or by itself as a vegetarian snack.
Serves 4

DEEP-FRIED SCOTCH EGGS

You will need:
This is a sure-fire winner as a picnic dish or a popular accompaniment to Sprout Curry.

$^1/_2$ kg pork sausagemeat
1 small onion peeled and finely chopped
1 x 5 ml tsp each of finely chopped fresh parsley, sage, mint and rosemary
4 eggs hard-boiled and shelled
Flour for coating
1 egg, beaten
Approx 175 g dried breadcrumbs
Oil for deep frying

1. Put the sausage meat, onion and mixed herbs together in a bowl and mix well.
2. Divide the mixture into four and press firmly around the hard-boiled eggs.
3. Roll in flour then dip in beaten egg.
4. Coat with the breadcrumbs, making sure that the sausage meat is evenly covered. Chill in the refrigerator for at least 1 hour before frying.
5. Heat the oil gently in a deep-fat fryer until it is hot enough to turn a stale bread cube golden in about 20-30

seconds. (180°-190° C/350°-370° F on a deep-fat frying thermometer). Fry the Scotch eggs two at a time for about 10 minutes until they are crisp and golden-brown.

6. Drain on absorbent kitchen paper and keep warm while frying the remaining two Scotch eggs. Drain, transfer to a hot serving platter and serve. Alternatively serve cold as a snack or with crisp green salad.

CHILLI BUTTY

The chilli can be made well in advance and indeed this recipe is a great way to use up leftovers.

You will need:
Cooking oil for frying
1 large onion, peeled and sliced
1 garlic clove, crushed with 1 x 2.5 ml salt
3/4 kg minced beef
1 x 5 ml chilli powder or to taste
1 x 396g can tomatoes

150 ml beef stock
1 x 5 ml spoon sugar
2 x 15 ml spoons tomato purée
Freshly ground black pepper
1 x 432 g can red kidney beans, drained and rinsed in cold
running water
Sliced white bread
Butter

1. Heat 2 tablespoons of oil in a large pan. Add the onion
and garlic and fry gently until golden.
2. Add the beef and chilli powder and fry until the meat
is well-browned, stirring constantly to taste and bring to
the boil.
3. Stir in the tomatoes, stock, sugar, tomato purée and
pepper to taste and bring to the boil. Lower the heat,
cover and simmer gently for 30 minutes, adding the
drained kidney beans 5 minutes before the end of the
cooking time. Adjust seasoning and serve immediately
sandwiched between slices of buttered bread.

TWELVE-EGG OMELETTE WITH BEER

You will need:
12 eggs, beaten
Salt and freshly ground black pepper
$^1/_2$ pint best bitter
2 tablespoons oil

1. Beat the beer into the beaten egg until foaming and frothy, adding salt and pepper to taste.
2. Heat the oil in a very large frying pan and pour in the mixture.
3. Cook for five minutes until the mixture has set then turn and cook for five minutes on the other side.
4. Serve piping hot with a crisp green salad.

Paddy the Irish cook was famous for his bean soup.
'I use exactly 239 beans,' he said.
'One more and it would be too farty.'

* Mother Bromcie would love you to send your farting recipes to her for comparison with her own culinary delights. Please forward them to me at my publisher's address.

FARTING ETIQUETTE

THE RULES

When I am out and about, many people, when hearing my name, ask me about farting etiquette. When, and when not, to drop one is a major problem that all of us at some time or other have to face up to. The most common concern and the question I am most frequently asked is, 'I have just started going out with someone and I want to know when is the best time to introduce flatulence into the relationship?'

Let's face it readers, we have all faced this problem at one time or another! Let me give you an example, and ladies, pardon me for giving this from the male perspective.

You have been dating a very refined lady for a few weeks. You have been out on the town a few times and have eaten at the best establishments your budget allows. There is one thing that is gnawing away at you and that is having to hold in the build-up of gas for fear of upsetting your date.

Some people I know start as they mean to go on and let rip from day one of a new relationship. I personally find this behaviour loutish and uncouth.

Farting has to be carefully introduced into a relationship to allow both parties the freedom to express themselves. I have listed some of the rules on etiquette to help readers through this social minefield.

• By about the fourth date you should now be relaxed in the company of each other. You now feel that the time is right to allow your partner to share with you what up till now has been held back for fear of rejection. Do not, reader, be tempted to let one rocket out which rattles the doors. From past experience I feel that the best way (and here you have to use some skill) is to let a delicate flower of a fart escape your cheeks. It must be loud enough for your date to hear. Now, here is the clever bit. Do not boast or show any pride in your fart, rather show horror and shame. At this point your partner will throw his/her arms around you and tell you not to worry. The ice is broken and both of you can now fart together with ease.

• Ladies, read the above and remember I have written this from a male point of view. The rule for a woman is, whatever you do, do not fart on a first date! Please – and I know this is sexist – let the man do it first. If you do thunder one out, his poor masculinity will be brought into question and the relationship will be doomed. The only exception to this rule is if you are a policewoman or a prison warden. In that case we males expect it!

• At this point I should bring up the subject of fanny farts. If the affair has already reached the point of freefall farting, then no problem! However, if it has not this may come as a great shock to some men. Ladies, fart warily and do try not to surprise him too soon. Men, should an involuntary rasp occur during lovemaking, be a man and neither recoil in horror – NOR laugh. Be sensitive to how your partner may be feeling and either ignore the parp or reassure your loved one. This way you can laugh long and loud about it with your mates for years to come. I have written a book on this very delicate subject called *Fanny Farts – Myth or Just Damn Rude?* for those that would like to know more on the subject.

• Lifts and enclosed spaces are a definite no-no. You might like the odour of your farts but others will not.

• Never fart near a fresh-food counter – not even an organic-food one.

I was once in a supermarket by the fresh-meat counter. Some villain had just unloaded a motherload of putrid pong. A lady nearby was heard to exclaim, 'Do not buy their meat, it has obviously gone off.'

• Never fart and then embrace your lover whilst wearing an overcoat on a cold day. As we know, hot air rises and your stench will travel upwards and emanate from beneath your coat lapels. Your embrace will be very short as the noxious substance hits your loved one's nostrils.

• Farting in bed (blanket ripping) and then pulling back the covers and sniffing one's own fart is a perfectly acceptable practice. However, pushing your loved one's head under (or Dutch-ovening) must rank as a crime against humanity! This is a very common male habit and I cannot stress enough that it is very unpleasant for the victim – I was once subjected to it by a policewoman.

• Never fart in the company of your mother-in-law/father-in-law.

• At work, never go into someone's office, drop one and then leave. This was done to me on numerous occasions by a certain gentleman. The odour would linger so much that people coming in an hour later would exclaim, 'Martin's in today then!'

• If you are the sole occupant of a bath then farting is to be encouraged as it is a cheap way of enjoying a jacuzzi. However, farting in a bath whilst sharing it is to be discouraged. The effect of the hot water on the lower intestines is such that you could end up firing out a gust of gas and worse. There is nothing more embarrassing than sharing your bath with your partner and something nasty.

• My last rule is the most important. You must take heed of this even if you ignore all my other rules. After six pints of beer and a chicken curry do not go to work wearing light coloured trousers. I am sure I do not need to spell it out for you. Your whole career could rest on keeping to this rule with complete fidelity.

ARE FARTS DANGEROUS?

Ill blows the wind that profits nobody.
WILLIAM SHAKESPEARE, HENRY VI

Better to burp and bear the shame than to squelch the belch and bear the pain.

ANONYMOUS

I often get asked if farting is dangerous. Actually farts are quite hygienic. They do not carry germs because the environment of the colon is acidic and any bacteria that do get through are harmless. So are farts dangerous? Here are my answers:

Yes: if working close to open flames. One student of mine very stupidly farted on to a camp fire and recorded a flame of over 1 metre.

Yes: if farting on to a lit match.
(DO NOT TRY THIS AT HOME.)

Yes: if inhaled at close range. Inhaling farts will gradually poison one causing light-headedness and headaches. So don't ride pillion on a motorcycle or hire a tandem if the person in front of you guzzled beans the night before.

Yes: if excessive. Gas in the intestine can cause considerable discomfort. It is commonly thought to cause abdominal pain, bloating, ballooning, distention, meteorism, voluminous abdomen, belching, or passage of excessively noxious farts.

Yes: if trapped. Farts sometimes don't do what they are supposed to, that is, come out of the bottom hole. Instead, gas builds up in the intestine. Trapped wind can be very painful, with the abdomen sometimes swelling so much that the sufferer may feel that they are going to explode.

Anyone in this condition should go straight to their doctor as diagnosis is vital. Do check first that:

a. You have not just eaten the contents of a fridge
b. That you do not have an obese beer belly and are making excuses
c. That you are not pregnant

Yes: during surgery. During digestive surgery or endoscopic surgery of the colon, sometimes the intestinal gas explodes in contact with the electric scalpel. The same may happen when the bowel is opened with the electric scalpel. In his book *The History of Farting*, Dr Benjamin Bart refers to a case in a hospital in Denmark in 1980. Surgeons were operating on a male patient. An electrical surgical knife, much favoured by modern surgeons because they cauterize small blood vessels as they go, ignited a pocket of intestinal gases. This set off an explosion which rippled its way through the poor fellow's digestive organs and, despite the best efforts of the surgeons to repair the damage, the patient died.

Yes: if you are a baby. Infants appear to pass an excessive amount of gas which may be an indication of colic.

Yes: if it comes out the wrong way. Swallowed air can

become trapped and may cause diffuse abdominal distension. Left upper quadrant fullness and pressure radiating to the left side of the chest may result. Relief comes when the burp finally manages to get out or when you finally let go a good old fart.

Yes: if held in for too long. After a few hours all that gas will be trying to enter your blood system and poison you, so it's not a good idea to try it.

Yes: if farting in an enclosed space. After farting repeatedly into the same room for several hours you may well experience a near-death experience. Reputedly, a man did once end his earthly days in such a pastime.

Yes: if you're a hypochondriac. Many people enjoy their farts in secret, but in public feel the need to affect a bowel or intestinal disorder rather than admitting that they ate curry the night before. They will talk of such thing as having a hypersensitive intestine or irritable bowel syndrome.

Curative measures:
- such products as Deflatine, Wind-Eze and Beano (US) which are available from your local chemist
- chalk tablets – available over the counter or from your GP
- pineapple – the Indians used to eat pineapple after a meal to aid digestion
- peppermints – may help to settle the stomach – hence the after-dinner mint
- let go of your hang-ups and just let them rip!

Preventative measures:
- Don't overindulge in Mrs Bromcie's sprout curry
- Avoid the foods listed on pages 31–34
- Don't exercise directly after a meal
- Don't become a vegetarian
- Don't go on a detox diet
- Chew your food
- Don't talk while eating
- Don't wear white underwear

DID YOU KNOW?
Research shows that most people who claim to fart excessively do not in fact do so more than those that can relax and enjoy an honest blow.

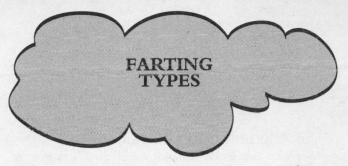

FARTING TYPES

It always amuses me to see how my first-year students record their findings. Here are some of my favourite examples:

TYPES OF FARTERS -
Research for end-of-year thesis.
Student 101X

He was a real fart smeller – uh, I mean, a real smart feller

THE AMBITIOUS FARTER:
One who's always in there first with a fart and quick to sniff out the competition.

THE BLANKET-RIPPING FARTER:
One who farts in bed and puts his head under the blanket to savour the smell.

THE COULDN'T-CARE-LESS FARTER:
One who farts loudly in board meetings, in lifts, during concerts and even at church.

THE DUTCH-OVEN FARTER:
One who farts in bed and then holds his partner's head under the bedclothes.

THE ENVIRONMENTAL FARTER:
One who worries that his farts are adding to air pollution.

THE FOOLISH FARTER:
One who suppresses a fart for hours and hours.

THE GHOULISH FARTER:
One who only farts in the dark.

THE HONEST FARTER:
One who openly admits he's farted.

THE IMPUDENT FARTER:
One who farts loudly and then laughs.

THE JELLY-BEAN FARTER:
According to Confucius, one who farts in technicolour.

THE KINETIC FARTER:
One who farts while walking or running.

THE LAZY FARTER:
One who merely fizzles.

THE MUSICAL FARTER:
'Tenor or bass, clear as a bell, smells like shit and sounds like hell.'

THE NOSY FARTER:
One who insists on sticking his nose into other people's farts.

THE OBSCENE FARTER
One who pulls down his trousers before farting.

THE PROUD FARTER:
One who thinks his farts are exceptionally pleasant.

THE QUEASY FARTER:
One who farts and feels sick at the smell.

THE RED-CARD FARTER:
One who is identified as having let out a particularly foul fart that warrants his immediate evacuation from the sports field, the changing-room, or any other public place.

THE SNORKEL FARTER:
One who farts in the bath or swimming pool and then looks around for the fish.

THE TIMID FARTER
One who jumps when he farts.

THE INCOMPETENT FARTER:
One who tries very hard to fart but shits himself instead.

THE VAIN FARTER:
One who loves the sound and smell of his own farts.

THE WILY FARTER:
One who observes great trickery or cunning in placing a fart where it gets blamed on other people.

THE XENOPHOBIC FARTER:
One who is afraid of farting in foreign places.

THE YIN/YANG FARTER:
One who tries to harmonize the positive and negative properties of a fart.

THE ZONKED FARTER:
One who has become drugged by the smell of his own farts.

TYPES OF FART –
Research for end-of-term paper.
Student 200X

There are only two kinds of farts:
1) Your own
2) Someone else's

ATOMIC FART: The atomic fart is incredibly loud and smells awful too. It also results in a big explosion, causing everyone to fall to the ground, suffering the effects of methane poisoning.

BABLER BAZOOKA FART (or the Redhill Ripper): The sort of fart that will wake you up at night because it smells so bad! They can be silent or noisy, but they are the most fetid, repulsive, smelliest farts imaginable. In Transylvania, legend has it even the undead are

repulsed by these. They're mostly dropped by women who try to keep them in, but it would be far better for all of us if they let rip frequently.

CHURCH FART: Picture the scene: you're sitting in church, you bend over to pick up a hymn book, and ...'PBBBBBBT'... a giant fart rips out. Fate dictates that you are sitting next to an old lady, who will stare down the pew, looking disgusted.

DELAYED-REACTION FART: You have the urge, but it goes away. You go on about your business and a few seconds, or longer, later, 'BBRRMMPHH'....

EBOLA FART: You are out with some of your friends. One of them farts and before you know it, farting breaks out everywhere.

FOLLOW-THROUGH FART: As Atomic fart, only this time the issuer does not have enough time to get to the bathroom.

GREEN-LIGHT FART: A fart where the conditions make it perfect for it to be released. This one can be as long and loud as the issuer can make it. It rarely occurs in lifts, cars, boardrooms or public places.

HAY FEVER FART: Basically, you fart when you sneeze, but the catch is that you can't smell it.

IRREPRESSIBLE INTERNAL FART: When you try to hold a fart in for too long, the Internal fart can be worse than the real thing (for you, not bystanders). It often sounds like heavy stomach growling. Not a true fart, but everyone knows that you will have to let it go soon. This fart will always make its way out eventually.

JAPANESE FART: In Japan, it is quite permissible to let rip at the dinner-table. So imagine, if you will, a family well satisfied after a fart-inducing meal, openly breaking wind together, unashamedly and with gusto!

KWEEEEEF FART: You are sitting in an orchestra with perfect posture when you let out a fart that sounds like a squeaking clarinet. Being in this musical environment, you can get away with such an emission.

LORD-OF-THE-DANCE FART: In an attempt to cover up the sound of a fart, you switch the topic of conversation to *Lord of the Dance* and start to stamp your feet loudly on the ground. Whilst you are doing this, you let one escape without anyone noticing.

MORNING FART: The 'first-thing-out-of-bed' fart. Long, loud and not too smelly; very satisfying to release all that gas after the night-time build-up.

MOURNING FART: The fart that lacks research as it has not been definitely proven that anyone died of a fart. Could be applied to anyone disrespectful enough to fart at someone's funeral or on their grave.

NINJA FART: A Ninja is a Japanese warrior trained in ninjutsu, the art of stealth or invisibility. A fart of the same name, therefore, describes a silent emission with a deadly odour.

ORGANIC FART: The person who farts an Organic fart is usually heavily into health foods and may even ask if you noticed how good, pure and healthy his fart smells. It may smell to you like any other fart, but there is no harm in agreeing with him. He is doing what he thinks is best.

PALMER FART: For years a guy I worked with used to walk into my office, drop one, then depart, shutting my door behind him. I would like his actions to be officially recognised and hereby enter him on to my list of farts. You know who you are!

QUESTIONING FART: This fart starts out low, and rises in pitch towards its conclusion, sounding as if your arse is asking a question.

RED-LIGHT FART: The fart that builds up but never happens alone. Hopefully identified by the issuer and held back.

SADDAM **H**USSEIN FART: (also known as 'the mother of all farts') Chemical warfare has begun. You should ring up CNN and send for United Nation inspectors owing to the huge scale of the potential outbreak.

TITANIC FART: This was the really huge fart you did when you were living with your parents. Even now you are grown up they keep reliving it to everyone you introduce them to. You start to think they might be going to sell the movie rights, and fantasize that Celine Dion will sing the theme song, 'My Fart Will Go On'.

UNDERWATER FART: Often done in the bath, or while swimming. It bears an uncanny resemblance to the sound made by the engine of a nuclear submarine. Can be smelt on rising to the surface, and experienced windbreakers will often catch the fart in an upturned jam-jar, in order to set light to it.

VIAGRA FART: After a long slow fart, you feel yourself aroused.

WEDDING FART: This fart occurs when the vicar pronounces the happy couple husband and wife. An eggy and beefy combination, as well as loud and deadly; when these are on the loose, the bride and groom are the last ones out of the church.

X-RATED FART: This is a fart of such horrifically smelly and sonorific proportions that it must never be aloud to escape in company; essentially a fart that must be emitted in complete privacy.

YOGIC FART: An inevitable by-product of athletic yogic positions and intense concentration. As both the mind and body are focused on supreme relaxation and control, one's ability to monitor the passage of internal gases becomes impaired, and the inevitable occurs

ZIGZAGGER FART: A particularly tricky and quite crafty emission, it never follows an obvious path. Rather it weaves and winds, meandering with purpose, making it impossible to know with certainty the true origins of the offending fart, and indeed to predict where the fart will come to rest.

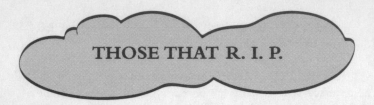

THOSE THAT R. I. P.

GREAT FARTS AND FARTERS OF HISTORY

> *Wherever you may be*
> *Always let your wind go free.*
> *I held mine and it done for me*
> *R.I.P.*
> ANONYMOUS

History is littered – or perhaps one should say punctuated – with farts, although a certain coyness on the part of biographers and historians means that a great many have been lost to later generations.

Robert Graves in *I, Claudius* tells how the eponymous Roman emperor (10 BC–AD 54; ruled AD 41–54), who invaded and conquered Britain in AD 43, would adjure family and friends and guests to let their wind go, rather than run the risk of harming the bowels. The embarrassing fart in the presence of some august personage is an enduring theme in farting histroy down the years; in *A Reed Shaken by the Wind*, his account of a journey among the marsh Arabs of Iraq in the company of the explorer Wilfred Thesiger, Gavin Maxwell repeats a tale told him by one of their hosts in a remote region: a young man farted at the Court of the Persian king, and immediately exiled himself from Court and country. Returning, an old, grey-bearded man, he was met at the frontier by a guard, who asked him in what year he had left the country. The old man told him the year, at which the guard laughed and said, 'Ah yes, that was the year So-and-So farted at Court.' The story has echoes, as the reader will see, of what befell Lord Oxford in the presence of Good Queen Bess, and also of one of the tales in what is popularly called *The Arabian Nights*, 'The Story of Abu Hasan'.

The fart also has a long and distinguished history as a literary device. The most famous farts in English literature are probably those in 'The Miller's Tale', from Geoffrey Chaucer's *The Canterbury Tales*, but one of the other stories is concerned solely with a fart. 'The Summoner's Tale' pillories a greedy friar trying to extract a legacy for himself and the twelve fellow members of his order from a dying man (the Summoner, angered by the Friar's tale, is anxious to have is revenge). Urged to reach behind the man to receive his inheritance, the friar, excited at the thought of what the legacy might be, fumbles round the dying man's backside and receives . . . a resounding fart. Having agreed that he will share his legacy fairly with his brethren, the rest of the tale concerns how the friar is to divide the sound and smell of the fart equally, a problem for which a solution is formulated by an ingenious squire. *The Canterbury Tales* date from the fourteenth century, but Chaucer was neither the first poet or writer, nor by any means the last, to pepper his work with farts: Robert Burns; James Joyce; Henry Fielding; Daniel Defoe; J. P. Donleavy; John Skelton; Henry Miller; John Wilmot, Earl of Rochester; Charles Sackville, Lord Buckhurst; George Villiers, Duke of Buckingham, and hundreds of other literary luminaries have all ruffled their pages with the passing of wind . . .

Bowing Out

In his *Brief Lives*, the English antiquary and biographer John Aubrey (1626-97) vividly describes the fate of the court poet Edward de Vere, seventeenth Earl of Oxford (1550-1604), after an embarrassing moment in the presence of the formidable Queen Elizabeth I:

> This Earl of Oxford, making of his low obeisance to Queen Elizabeth, happened to let a Fart, at which he was so abashed and ashamed that he went to travel, 7 years. On his return the Queen welcomed him home, and said, 'My Lord, I has forgot the Fart.'

The Story of Abu Hasan

The story of Abu Hasan appears in Sir Richard Burton's translation of *The Book of the Thousand Nights and a Night*, otherwise known as *The Arabian Nights Entertainments*, and was privately published in 1885. His version is as follows:

Abu Hasan was an opulent merchant. His wife died when both were still young and his friends urged him to marry again. Abu Hasan duly entered into negotiations with a maid of great beauty. The wedding banquet was a great celebration and everyone was invited. 'The whole house was thrown open to feasting: there were rices of five different colours, and sherbets of as many more; and kid goats stuffed with walnuts, almonds and pistachios; and a young camel roasted whole. So they ate and drank and made mirth and merriment; and the bride was displayed in her seven dresses.'

Eventually the bridegroom was summoned to the chamber where his bride sat enthroned, and he rose slowly and with dignity from his divan; but as he did so, 'because he was overfull of meat and drink, lo and behold! he brake wind, great and terrible. Thereupon each guest turned to his neighbour and talked aloud, and made as though he has heard nothing.' Abu Hasan, however, was terribly embarrassed. Instead of going to the bridal chamber he went down to the courtyard, saddled his horse and rode to the harbour, where he boarded a ship about to sail to India. There he remained for ten years, but at the end of that time 'he was seized with homesickness, and the longing to behold his native land was that of a lover pining for his beloved; and he came near to die of yearning desire.' Abu Hasan returned secretly to his native land, disguised in rags 'But when he drew near his old home, he looked down upon it from the hills with brimming eyes, and said to himself, "There is a chance that they might know thee; so I will wander about the outskirts and hearken to the folk. Allah grant that what happened to me be not remembered by them."

'He listened carefully for seven nights and seven days, till it so chanced that, as he was sitting at the door of a hut, he heard the voice of a young girl saying. "O my mother, tell me the day when I was born, for one of my companions is about to tell my fortune." And the mother answered, "Thou was born, O my daughter, on the very night when Abu Hasan brake wind."'

When Abu Hasan heard these words 'he rose up from the bench and fled, saying to himself, "Verily thy breaking of wind hath become a date, which shall last for ever and ever."' He returned to India and remained in exile for the rest of his life.

Edward Lear

Edward Lear (1812-88), the nineteenth-century English artist, traveller and writer, now best known for his works for children, and especially his *Book of Nonsense* and its successors, wrote affectionately of a favourite farting duchess who gave enormous dinner parties attended by the cream of society. One night she delivered a fart of such epic proportions that it simply could not be ignored. Quick as a flash she turned her gaze upon her stoic butler standing behind her and cried 'Hawkins, stop that.' To which he replied 'Certainly, Your Grace. Which way did it go?'

Le Pétomane

The first man to make a living from breaking wind in public was a French entertainer – if that's the right word – Joseph Pujol (1857-1945). His stage title was 'Le

Pétomane', and his act took him from provincial fleapits to Paris, to the Moulin Rouge itself. He discovered his strange talent at an early age and first turned it into entertainment in the 1880s. His debut at the Moulin Rouge came in 1892 and was an overnight success. After all, how many people can imitate gunfire, smoke cigarettes, play tunes on a tin flute, and sound like mock bugle calls? It was said of him that Sarah Bernhardt drew box-office receipts of 8,000 francs, but Le Pétomane in a single Sunday took 20,000 francs at the box office. He could even fart the opening bars of the French national anthem.

Rarely has this usually distressing symptom been turned to such advantage. Pujol became affluent as an effluent performer, and died in 1945 at what, by any standards, has to be considered a ripe old age.

A letter to the Royal Academy of Brussels from Benjamin Franklin

Benjamin Franklin (1706-90), the American statesman, scientist and writer, and one of the fathers of the Declaration of Independence that secured the colonies' independence from Britain, was a man of wide knowledge and an enquiring turn of mind, as this tongue-in-cheek letter from 1780 clearly shows. For although Franklin is well known for his electrical experiments using kites to attract lightning, it is wind of a different kind that concerns him here, offering advice that seems at times to echo the Emperor Claudius.

GENTLEMEN:
I have perus'd your late mathematical prize Question, propos'd in lieu of one in Natural Philosophy for the ensuing Year, viz: 'Une Figure quelconque donnée, on demande d'y inscrire le plus grand nombre de Fois

possible une autre Figure plus petite quelconque, qui est aussi donnée.'

I was glad to find by these following words, 'L'Académie a juge que cette Découverte, en étendant les Bornes de nos Connoissances, ne seroit pas sans Utilité,' that you esteem utility an essential point in your enquiries, which has not always been the case with all Academies; & I conclude therefore that you have given this question instead of a philosophical, or, as the learned express it, a physical one, because you could not at the Time think of a physical one that promis'd greater Utility.

Permit me then humbly to propose one of that sort for your consideration, and thro' you, if you approve it, for the serious enquiry of learned Physicians, Chemists, etc., of this enlighten'd Age.

It is universally well known, that in digesting our common Food, there is created or produced in the Bowels of human creatures, a great quantity of Wind.

That the permitting this Air to escape and mix with the Atmosphere, is usually offensive to the Company, from the fetid Smell that accompanyes it.

That all well-bred People therefore, to avoid giving such offense, forcibly restrain the Efforts of Nature to discharge that Wind.

That so retained contrary to Nature, it not only gives frequently great present Pain, but occasions future Diseases such as habitual Cholics, Ruptures, Tympanies, &c., often destructive of the Constitution, and sometimes of Life itself.

Were it not for the odiously offensive Smell accompanying such escapes, polite People would probably be under no more Restraint in discharging such Wind in Company, than they are in spitting or in blowing their Noses.

MY PRIZE QUESTION THEREFORE SHOULD BE: To discover some Drug, wholesome and not disagreeable, to be mixed with our common Food, or Sauces, that shall render the natural discharges of Wind from our Bodies not only inoffensive, but agreeable as Perfumes.

That this is not a chimerical Project and altogether impossible, may appear from these considerations. That we already have some knowledge of the Means capable of varying that Smell. He that dines on stale Flesh, especially with much Addition of onions, shall be able to afford a stink that no company can tolerate; while he that has liv'd for some time on Vegetables only, shall have that Breath so pure as to be insensible to the most delicate Noses; and if he can manage so as to avoid the Report, he may anywhere give vent to his Griefs, unnoticed. But as there are many to whom an entire Vegetable diet would be inconvenient, and as a little quick Lime thrown into a Jakes will correct the amazing Quantity of fetid air arising from the vast Mass of putrid Matter contain'd in such Places, and render it rather pleasing to the Smell, who knows but that a little Powder of Lime (or some other thing equivalent) taken in our Food, or perhaps a Glass of lime water drank at Dinner, may have the same effect on the Air produc'd in and issuing from our Bowels? This is worth the Experiment. Certain it is also that we have the power of changing by slight means the Smell of another discharge, that of our Water. A few stems of Asparagus eaten, shall give our Urine a disagreeable Odour; and a Pill of Turpentine no bigger than a Pea, shall bestow on it the pleasing smell of violets. And why should it be thought more impossible in Nature, to find Means of making a Perfume of our Wind than of our Water?

For the Encouragement of this Enquiry (from the immortal Honour to be reasonably expected by the Inventor) let it be considered of how small Importance to Mankind, or to how small a Part of Mankind have been useful those Discoveries in Science that have heretofore made Philosophers famous. Are there twenty Men in Europe this day the happier, or even the easier for any Knowledge they have pick'd out of Aristotle? What comfort can the Vortices of Descartes give to a Man who has Whirlwinds in his Bowels! The knowledge of Newton's Mutual Attraction of the particles of matter, can it afford ease to him who is rack'd by their mutual Repulsion, and the cruel Distentions it occasions? The pleasure arising to a few Philosophers, from seeing, a few times in their Lives, the threads of Light untwisted and separated by the Newtonian Prism into seven Colours, can it be compar'd with the Ease and Comfort every Man living might feel seven times a day, by discharging freely the Wind from his Bowels? Especially if it be converted into a Perfume; for the Pleasures of one Sense being little inferior to those of another, instead of pleasing the Sight, he might delight in the Smell of those about him, and make numbers happy, which to a benevolent Mind must afford infinite Satisfaction. The generous Soul, who now

80

endeavours to find out whether the Friends he enter-tains like best Claret or Burgundy, Champagne or Madeira, would then enquire also whether they choose Musk or Lilly, Rose or Bergamot, and provide accordingly. And surely such a Liberty of ex-pressing one's Scent-i-ments, & pleasing one another, is of infi-nitely more importance to human Happiness than that Liberty of the Press, or of abusing one another, which the English are so ready to fight and die for.

In short, this Invention, if completed, would be, as Bacon expresses it, 'Bringing philosophy home to men's Business and Bosoms'. And I cannot but con-clude, that in comparison therewith for universal and continual Utility, the Science of the Philosophers aforemention'd, even with the addition, Gentlemen, of your 'figure quelconque', and the Figures inscrib'd in it, are, all together, scarcely worth a FART-HING.

Reforming zeal

Philip Schwarzerd, the sixteenth-century German religious and educational reformer known as 'Melancthon' (a rendering in Greek of his German surname, which means 'black earth'), was one of the principal associates and helpers of Martin Luther, the leader of the Protestant Reformation. According to Melancthon, when Luther encountered the Devil and trounced him in argument, 'the Demon departed . . . after having emitted a crepitation of no small size, which left a train of foul odour in the chamber for several days afterwards'. During another discussion with Old Nick, the Great Reformer, finding his arguments this time to be of no avail, confounded his enemy 'mit einem Furz' (with a fart). The image of Luther nowadays is perhaps that of a rather stern and even puritan evangelist, although he was unquestionably a spiritual genius. But in fact he was a man of great human warmth, and one blessed with a robust, at times even rather coarse, sense of humour, as is shown by a remark he made to a guest at the end of a meal they had shared: 'Warum rülpset und pfurzet Ihr nicht? Hat es Euch nicht geschmecket?' ('Why don't you belch and fart? Was it not to your taste?')

Revolting peasants?

Luther's trouncing of the Devil was not the first time the Forces of Darkness had been confronted, and confounded, by flatulence. A French tale from the fourteenth century, *Le Pet au vilain* (*The Peasant's Fart*), has Satan once more discomfited by an ill wind. A peasant was suffering so acutely from indigestion that the Devil, believing the man was going to die, sent one of his minions to catch the poor man's soul in a sack as he expired. The peasant, however, farted hugely instead, straight into the sack. Thinking to have trapped another soul, the minion dashed back to Hell with his prize. On opening the sack, however, the most vile smell imaginable filled what is, by any account, a pretty vile-smelling place – with the result that from then on French peasants have never gone to Hell. Or so it is said . . .

Elevated courtiers

In more elevated circles, the late Lord Adeane (1910–84), who, as Sir Michael Adeane, was Private Secretary to the Queen from 1953 until his retirement in 1972, was a man famed for his wit as well as for the graceful tact without which no such courtier can last for long. On one occasion at Buckingham Palace he excused himself to a colleague, saying that he had to take a party of proctologists (specialists in matters affecting the rectum, if you must know) for an audience with the Sovereign.

'What on earth are proctologists?' his friend asked.

'Bottom doctors, my dear chap – bottom doctors,' Adeane replied gaily.

'Good heavens! How ghastly! How on earth will you introduce them to Her Majesty?'

'Simple – I shall say they are fundamentalists.'

Fair Stood the Wind for France

The French novelist Honoré de Balzac (1799-1850), author of the great collection of novels under the general title *La Comédie humaine* which includes *Eugénie Grandet*, *Le Père Goriot* and *La Cousine Bette*, is said to have remarked: 'I should like one of these days to be so well known, so popular, so celebrated, so famous, that it would permit me . . . to break wind in society, and society would think it a most natural thing.' The strain of robust coarseness in his work - indeed, in Balzac himself - caused much fuss in his day, and scandalized some members of the literary establishment.

Heartburn

> Love is the fart
> Of every heart,
> It pains a man when kept close,
> And others doth offend, when 'tis let loose.

It is difficult to believe that this grotesque notion was enshrined in verse by a man described by *The Oxford Companion to English Literature* as 'one of the most elegant and brilliant of the Cavalier poets'. Nevertheless, these lines are to be found in 'Love's Offence', a poem by Sir John Suckling (1609-42), one of the leaders of the Royalist faction in the early days of King Charles I's troubles with Parliament, and a man famed for his gaiety, wit, extravagance, and love of gaming. Forced to flee to France during the Civil War, Suckling is – according to Aubrey's *Brief Lives* – said to have committed suicide there; the same source also credits him with inventing the card game cribbage, although he is probably best remembered nowadays for his line, 'Why so pale and wan, fond lover?' It is, frankly, not at all difficult to imagine why any mistress of Suckling's might have been pale and wan, especially given seventeenth-century diet and standards of 'personal hygiene'.

WISE WORDS
ON WIND

My students know that I always have a quotation at my fingertips for every occasion (if it's to do with farting). Here are just a few of them – some of the wisest words ever spoken on the subject . . .

Full of sound and fury, signifying nothing.

WILLIAM SHAKESPEARE, MACBETH

Quando il malato scoppia, il medico plange!
(When the sick man farts, the doctor cries –
an old saying from southern Italy, akin to
the English saying 'An apple a day keeps
the doctor away.')

A fabis abstinentes (Eat no beans)
PYTHAGORAS

A man may break a word with you, sir; and words are but wind; Ay; and break it in your face, so he break it not behind.
WILLIAM SHAKESPEARE, THE COMEDY OF ERRORS

For the gentle wind does move / Silently, invisibly.
WILLIAM BLAKE

May the wind be always at your back.
ANONYMOUS

All citizens shall be allowed to
pass gas whenever necessary.
CLAUDIUS CAESAR

This too shall pass...
ABRAHAM LINCOLN

What comfort can the vortices of Descartes
give to a man who has
whirlwinds in his bowels?

BENJAMIN FRANKLIN

It is best for flatulence to pass without noise
and breaking, though it is better for it to pass
with noise than to be intercepted and
accumulated internally.

HIPPOCRATES, C. 460–C. 357 BC

What winde can there blowe,
that doth not some man please?
A fart in the blowyng
doth the blower ease.

JOHN HEYWOOD

A voice within us speaks the startling word.

RICHARD HENRY DANA, 1833

Through perils both of wind and limb,
Through thick and thin she follow'd him.

SAMUEL BUTLER, HUDIBRAS

Blow, winds, and crack your cheeks!
rage! blow!
WILLIAM SHAKESPEARE, KING LEAR

Who has seen the wind?
Neither you nor I:
But when the trees bow down their heads,
The wind is passing by.
CHRISTINA ROSSETTI, WHO HAS SEEN THE WIND?

92

'The story is like the wind,' the Bushman prisoner said. 'It comes from a far-off place, and we feel it.'

LAURENS VAN DER POST, A STORY LIKE THE WIND

Mock on, mock on, Voltaire, Rousseau;
Mock on, mock on; 'tis all in vain!
You throw the sand against the wind,
And the wind blows it back again.

WILLIAM BLAKE, MOCK ON, MOCK ON,

VOLTAIRE, ROUSSEAU

Absence is to love what wind is to fire; it extinguishes the small, it enkindles the great.

COMTE DE BUSSY-RABUTIN,
HISTOIRE AMOUREUSE DES GAULES

Nullius addictus iurare in verba magistri,
Quo me cumque rapit tempestas, deferor hospes.
(Not bound to swear allegiance to any master,
Wherever the wind takes me I travel as a visitor.)

HORACE, **EPISTLES**

Oaths are but words, and words but wind.

SAMUEL BUTLER, **HUDIBRAS**

94

They that sow the wind
shall reap the whirlwind.
G.W. CURTIS, PUTNAM'S MAGAZINE

Big fires flare up in a wind, but little ones
are blown out unless they are carried in
under cover.
ST FRANCES DE SALES, INTRODUCTION À LA VIE DÉVOTÉ

In the bleak mid-winter
Frosty wind made moan . . .
CHRISTINA ROSSETTI, MID-WINTER

I have forgot much . . .
. . . gone with the wind . . .

ERNEST DOWSON, NON SUM QUALIS ERAM

Still as they run they look behind,
They hear a voice in every wind,
And snatch a fearful joy.

THOMAS GRAY, THE PROGRESS OF POESY

Surprised by joy – impatient as the Wind . . .

WILLIAM WORDSWORTH, SURPRISED BY JOY

96

Not I, not I, but the wind that blows through me!

D.H. LAWRENCE, SONG OF A MAN WHO HAS COME THROUGH

Blow the wind never so fast,
It will fall at last.

SPURGEON, JOHN PLOUGHMAN

There's no weather ill when the wind is still.

CAMDEN, REMAINS

The wind keeps not only in one quarter.
JOHN RAY, ENGLISH PROVERBS

Winds at night are always bright;
But winds in the morning, sailors
take warning.
WEATHER LORE

You can't catch the wind in a net.
SPURGEON, PLOUGHMAN PICTURES

All this wind shakes no corn.
HEYWOOD, **PROVERBS**

The wind in a man's face makes him wise.
S. PALMER, **MORAL ESSAYS ON PROVERBS**

What wind blew you hither?
GEOFFREY CHAUCER, **TROILUS AND CRISEYDE**

When the wind's in the north,
You mustn't go forth.

DENHAM, PROVERBS

Trace in the sky the painter's brush,
Then winds around you soon will rush.

WEATHER LORE

The wind flapped loose, the wind was still,
Shaken out dead from tree and hill:
I had walked on at the wind's will, –
I sat now, for the wind was still.

DANTE GABRIEL ROSSETTI, THE WOODSPURGE

I will not permit thirty men to travel four hundred miles to agitate a bag of wind.

ANDREW DICKSON WHITE, US EDUCATIONALIST

I should like one of these days to be so well known, so popular, so celebrated, so famous, that it would permit me ... to break wind in society, and society would think it a most natural thing.

HONORÉ DE BALZAC, FRENCH NOVELIST

101

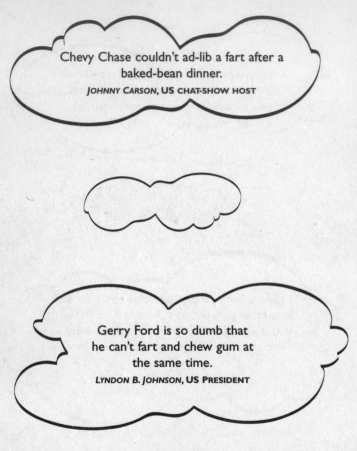

Chevy Chase couldn't ad-lib a fart after a baked-bean dinner.

JOHNNY CARSON, US CHAT-SHOW HOST

Gerry Ford is so dumb that he can't fart and chew gum at the same time.

LYNDON B. JOHNSON, US PRESIDENT

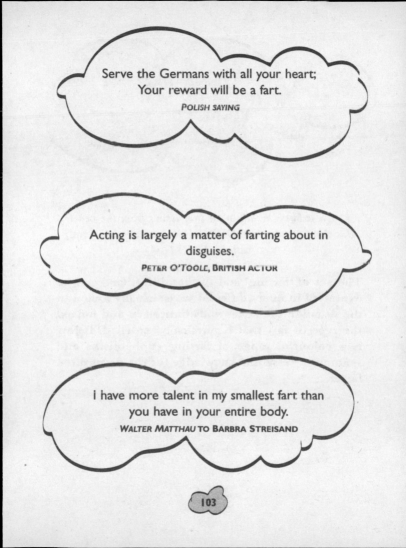

Serve the Germans with all your heart;
Your reward will be a fart.

POLISH SAYING

Acting is largely a matter of farting about in disguises.

PETER O'TOOLE, BRITISH ACTOR

I have more talent in my smallest fart than you have in your entire body.

WALTER MATTHAU TO BARBRA STREISAND

IT'S STILL A FART WHATEVER YOU CALL IT

A sigh is but a breath of air that issues from the heart;
But when it takes a DOWNWARD course, it's simply
called a FART!

The act of 'farting' and the resulting 'fart' can be expressed in many different ways; usually linked to the situation the farter finds himself in and indeed the type of fart that is physically expelled. Below is a colourful range of farting euphemisms and synonyms – essential knowledge for the committed farter.

TO FART (vb)

Backfire
Bark
Bip
Blast
Blow off
Blow the ol' butt trumpet
Break wind
Breeze
Cough
Crack a rat
Cut the cheese
Draw mud
Drop a shoe
Drop one's guts
Fire a Scud missile
Flatulate
Float an air biscuit
Fluff
Frame
Grep
Guff
Honk
Janet
Let off
Let one rip

Ming
Open one's lunch box
Pass wind
Pier
Poop
Pot
Proof
Queef
Rosebud
Rumble
Shoot a bunny
Step on a duck
Totter
Trump
Woof

FART/FARTING (n.)

Afterburner
Anal airwaves
Anal audio
Barking spider
Bench warmer
Bottom burp
Botty burp
Buck snort
Butt burner

Butt blast
Butt sneeze
Cheek flapper
Cheeser
Crack splitter
Disappointment from down under
Exploding turd
Explosion
Faecal fluffy
Firecracker
Flatulence
Gravy pants
Great brown cloud
Happy honker
Heinz burp
Hotty
Mud cricket
Mud duck
Natural gas
Nature's little surprise
Nature's musical box
One turd honking at another for right of way!
Pant stains
Panty burp
Prelude to shit
Pull my finger

Quakers – 9.5 on the rectal scale!
Raspberry tart
Rat bark
Ripper
S.A.V. – Silent and violent
S.B.D. – Silent but deadly
Shit siren
Shit snore
Sidewinder
Sneeze from the turtle's head
Stinker
Stinky
Thunder from down under
Tree frog
Trouser cough
Trouser ghost
Trouser ripper
Turd slamming on the brakes
Turd tootie
Under thunder
Wet one

FARTERS ANONYMOUS: TRUE FARTING CONFESSIONS

Not I, not I, but the wind that blows through me!

D. H. LAWRENCE

This year has been another fruitful one at Farters Anonymous. The following are first-hand farting stories related by students enrolled on my 'How To Let Go Of Your Farts' course, one of the many available at Farters Anonymous.

Hello, my name is Madeline and I am a farter. As a responsible junior-school teacher I usually give my class a word to learn each day so that the children will have a good vocabulary in later years. However, I sometimes wonder if the project is such a good idea. For example, last month we were trying to explain the correct use of the word 'definitely'. To make sure the students had a good understanding of the word, I asked them to put it in a sentence. A bright little girl volunteered 'The sky is definitely blue.' I pointed out that sometimes it is grey and cloudy so that it isn't 'definitely' blue. Another child then came up with 'grass is definitely green' to which I gave the same sort of answer. There was a long silence and just as I was about to give them some examples of my own, one of my pupils (I won't mention any names) called out 'Do farts have lumps?' Naturally, I was a bit irked but replied 'No,' and tried to move off the topic as fast as possible. However, he then burst into tears and sobbed, 'Well, I definitely have lumps in my pants.' As the class dissolved into laughter I rushed the offending child out of the room.

MADELINE M, MELBOURNE

110

Hello, my name is Jane and my husband is a farter. One night my husband (after a vicious curry) had really bad wind. Normally, I think this kind of thing is amusing but on this particular evening I was feeling a bit queasy after too many tequila slammers. I told him that if he did it one more time I was going to throw up. He did not heed my warning and let out an enormous nasty fart. That was it! I ran to our sliding glass door with my hand over my mouth. The entire contents of my stomach were deposited on to our back garden and as I was laughing so much I wet my pants. The next morning my husband went out to cut the grass and stepped right in my sick. He was not best pleased but I thought it poetic justice for ignoring me.

JANE H, BERKHAMSTED

Hello, my name is Donald and I am a farter. A friend of mine and I used to amuse ourselves by farting in public places, loud enough for others to hear, but delivered in such a way that no one could identify the guilty party. One time we were playing our game in a cinema. It was only about half-full so we sat a few seats apart from each other and went to work, calling back and forth to each other. The timing and sphincter control was amazing to behold as we released little portions about every 5 to 10 minutes. Heads were turning at first, but nobody was certain of what they were hearing, as if in denial. As the show went on, our farts were followed by bursts of laughter from the audience, and we struggled to stifle our own laughter. It was becoming like a contest to see who could pull off the loudest and the longest, while maintaining anonymity. Going for the trophy, I began to unleash the mother lode. It turned out to be a real freak of nature, but by the time I realised its impending fury, I was laughing so hard that I couldn't pinch it off. It was sounding off like a duck in an opera, and before I was halfway through the whole theatre had homed in on my position. The place was in an uproar. We ran out the back and missed the rest of the movie.

DONALD MCI, LIVINGSTONE

Hello, my name is Rachel and I am a farter. When I was six – yes I haven't forgotten it, it was so embarrassing – we were all made to sit cross-legged on a mat during class registration. Well, my mother had given me beans for my tea the night before and my stomach was feeling rather gassy. Suddenly, I knew I was in trouble – I was going to fart, so I uncrossed my legs and squeezed my buttocks together as hard as I could. The teacher looked over from her desk and thought that I was misbehaving. 'Over there in the corner,' she bellowed. 'Now!' she continued as I failed to move. Of course, as I stood up, all the air that I'd been holding in escaped in an enormous rush. There was a moment of shocked silence and then the class erupted in peals of laughter. The teacher was by now purple with fury and when we went into morning assembly in the school hall, she made me stand up all the way through whilst everyone else was seated. Naturally, all the school wanted to know why I had been singled out. It took me a few weeks to live it down but my prayers were answered when the teacher left the school shortly afterwards to humiliate other little kids elsewhere.

RACHEL Y, BRISBANE

Hello, my name is Suzanne and I am a farter. I'm 26 years old now. When I was about 15, my 13-year-old brother didn't believe that farts were flammable. So I set out to prove to him that they were. It was a Saturday morning, and we were laying about watching *Tiswas* on the TV. I had a Bic lighter handy, because I knew it wouldn't take long to prove my point. A few minutes later I felt a monster fart gurgling in my gut. I rolled on to my side, and got the lighter into position about an inch from my underwear, right above the launch tunnel. As the fart started coming out, I flicked the Bic. Then I saw a flame roll up over my side, and the fuzz on the carpet started burning. I rolled over the fire to put it out, and my brother started laughing so hard, his eyes were watering, and he had snot hanging off his face. After I saw that everything was OK, I busted out laughing too. Our mum came into the room asking what was so funny and what was that burning smell? Needless to say neither one of us could answer or move off the floor for quite a while. By the way, kids, I did burn a hole in my undies and singed a lot of hair off of my ass and side. DON'T DO IT !!!

SUZANNE P, TOOTING, LONDON

Hello, my name is Ted and I am a farter. I was picking up my date one evening, it was cold outside and I had on a long trench coat. I knew I had to let one go, so before I rang the door bell I let it fly. Well, just as I was about to ring the bell she opened the door and was ready to go. I walked her to the car, opened her door and helped her inside. I walked around and got in. I opened my coat when I sat down behind the wheel and out came the remains of my fart. With the long coat on and the cold temperature outside the door it had remained under the coat for us to enjoy. I looked at her as if she had done it. A man's got to do what a man's got to do.

TED F, UCKFIELD, SUSSEX

Hello, my name is Caroline and I am a farter. A few years ago when I was still living at home I decided to sneak into my grandfather's house with my man to get a bit of privacy. It was around two in the morning and the street was as quiet as the graveyard. We had been drinking copious amounts of beer and I had been letting rip for the last hour with some melodic farts. However, as it was so quiet I had been holding back but as we came to the door I suddenly let out a really loud fart which sounded like a car screeching to a halt. It made my bloke jump and the look of panic on his face set me about laughing so much I started letting go with short farts which sounded like a machine gun. My boyfriend looked at me and said, 'You are one nasty chick.' This made me laugh hysterically, which got the people across the road opening their front door threating to call the police. We beat a hasty retreat back to my parents, laughing all the way.

CAROLINE B, REDHILL

Hello, my name is David and I am a NOT a farter. When I was about 12 or 13 years old I went to the bus depot to catch a bus into the centre of Dundee. I went and sat on the top deck towards the back and waited for the bus to start its engine and get going. There was a man in front of me and about ten other people on the bus. The only noise was the odd cough or sneeze. Suddenly the guy directly in front of me let rip with a monster fart of nuclear proportions. Starting from the front of the bus my fellow passengers looked round to see who the culprit was. Imagine my horror when the perpetrator of this foul deed looked round at me! I could only do likewise and turn round and to my horror saw no one sat behind me. When I turned back the entire top deck looked at me with looks of disgust apart from the swine who did it. He looked at me and smirked. The only option open to me was to flee the bus and catch the next one. Thirty years later the humiliation and shame still comes back to haunt me every time I get on a bus. Why had I not said something to my fellow passengers? Why did I run?

DAVID C, DORKING

Hello, my name is Yvette and I am a farter. One night as I was preparing for bed by brushing my teeth in the bathroom, I stopped by my parents' room to hear my father's snoring which was always worth a listen. As he began to get louder and louder I just shook my head and wondered how anyone could sleep with that. All of a sudden, a fart came out loud enough to wake the dead and my dad let out one of those my-sleep–got–interrupted snorts. My mum also woke up and thought it was thunder outside. My dad blamed her, which was rich. I laughed so much I could not get to sleep for hours. My dad still insists he does not snore. My mum and I still joke about it.

YVETTE C, DOLLIS HILL, LONDON

Hello, my name is James and I am a farter. I have always had a problem with my bowels. My mother took me to the doctor's at quite a young age, to see if there was anything that could be done. I am sure the diet of baked beans and cottage cheese did not help but ...This story relates to a night about five years ago. I had been out with friends and was slightly the worse for wear. I was walking back to the place I was staying, and thought that I would just pop out a cheeky one. All of a sudden there was this torrent coming from my arse. Luckily, I was wearing cowboy boots so none came out the bottom. Anyway, I waddled home only to remember that I had to be up early the next morning, and the jeans I was wearing were the only ones I had with me. I popped them in the washing machine, but the mixed smell of damp and shit on the train the next morning, was unbearable. As for the boots, well suffice it to say that I did not brush my teeth the next morning.

JAMES P, FULHAM, LONDON

Hello, my name is Bob and I am a farter. I have quite a reputation for amusing uncouth behaviour but farting is one of my specialities. Once I was getting out of the shower and my wife Pam was in the bathroom talking to me. I felt a powerful fart building and asked her to inspect my arse, saying that I thought I had a cut back there. As soon as her face was near my arse I let loose with a long, wet, resounding blast that sounded extra special within the confines of our tiny bathroom. I feel that I must inform you that this will be the last time I tell this story, as I have just been informed by Pam that it is 'No longer funny'.

BOB C, SALISBURY

Hello, my name is George and I am a farter. I was selling appliances to Filipino nurses working in Saudi Arabia, where rules prohibit male guests from entering ladies' housing without an escort from management. Demonstrating the features of a stereo from the floor because there was no desk where the equipment could be laid on, my prospect, fresh and immaculate in her white uniform, stooped for a closer look. As she bent, a long high-pitched whistle came from her behind catching me and my huge Nigerian escort petrified. We all stared at each other as the poor girl's pretty face turned bright red. Quick as a flash I said 'That's a nice singing pair of pants you are wearing. I wish I had them. Where could I buy some?' We all had a good laugh and it was not long before I got to inspect her knickers more closely. But that's another story.

GEORGE McK, EDINBURGH

Hello, my name is [withheld] and I am a farter. My office was on the ground floor of a large West London publisher. As my car was parked in the underground car park I was in the habit of taking the lift down one floor to get to my car. This particular day was much like any other day apart from one thing – I had eaten a Thai green curry for lunch and it was producing a build-up of gas of El Niño proportions. I decided to leave for the day and as I made my way through the reception area towards the lift I felt an urgent need to let fly a big one. I could not drop one in reception as they would be aware it was me. Clenching my cheeks together I just made it to the lift. As the doors shut I let go a long hot fart which immediately filled the lift with a stench of grotesque proportions! The bad news was that in all the panic to let rip I had pressed +1 instead of –1. Instead of going down the lift went up. Fear and panic swept over me. I was trapped in a nightmare of my own making! Waving my arms about furiously I desperately tried to minimise the smell of my fart. It was no use, and as the door opened on the first floor, to my horror I saw three women from the marketing department getting in. They were all talking animatedly about some film or other but as the doors shut the full effects of my noxious gas hit their nostrils like a speeding car hitting a brick wall! They stopped talking and covered their noses with their hands. I am used to my smells and take some pride in my gas but these poor women had probably never come across a grandmaster like me before. As the doors opened on the ground floor they ran out of the lift gasping for air as they had been holding their breath. The lift carried on down to the car park and I drove home knowing it would be all round the office the next day. From that day to this I have never farted in a lift.

ANONYMOUS, KIDLINGTON, OXFORD

Hello, my name is Katharine and I am NOT a farter. I am here because when we go away on holiday, my family always seem to spend the whole time farting, or talking about farting. My family recently went on a two-week skiing holiday to Courcheval. Having failed to impress the chalet girl, during the first week of our stay, my brother and his friend tried their luck with chatting up the girls in a neighbouring resort – without much success. Then, finally, they came home one night claiming to have pulled two 'stunners' in a local bar. The rest of the night they stayed up drinking beer with my father, my husband and my sister's husband. The next morning they were all somewhat hung-over, to say the least. After a breakfast of eggs and porridge, the effects of their over-indulgence were really catching up on them, so you can imagine that by the time they were in the gondola lift going up to the slopes, they were farting away like troopers, making a right stink and blaming each other for the bad air conditions. Such was the appalling odour in the lift that my sister and I jumped out at the half-way station, while the men took the opportunity of the gust of fresh air that the opening doors let in to let off a few more farts. As we got out, two pretty girls jumped into our vacated seats with enthusiastic greetings to my brother and his friend. I think 'Hi!' was probably the last word they said. Needless to say, the girls weren't mentioned again, and the boys passed on boiled eggs, if not beer, after that.

KATHARINE G, MAIDENHEAD

All names have been changed. However, do feel free to send your true farting stories to me at my publishers or at: alec.bromcie@michaelomarabooks.com. Your story may appear in a future edition. We will let you know if we are going to use it.

FARTING LIMERICKS
by Helen Blowers

There was an old lady from Crewe
Who was constantly stricken with 'flu.
She'd cough herself hoarse
And sneeze with such force,
That she'd often let off a few too!

There is a young yachtsman from Wales,
Whose boating technique never fails.
He dines on baked beans
And plenty of greens,
So his farts put the wind in his sails.

There was an old geezer from Devon
Who'd fart on the stroke of eleven.
With baked beans for brunch
And poached eggs for lunch,
He'd be parping till quarter-past seven.

NO LAUGHING MATTER:
The best farting jokes around!

I couldn't resist lowering the tone of this book by sharing with readers some of my favourite farting jokes of all time – and, just like a fart, the best ones hang around the longest. Honk as loud as you like!

How can you tell if a woman is wearing tights?
If she farts her ankles blow up.

Why do farts smell?
So deaf people can enjoy them too.

Three guys were on a plane. The first guy said, 'I'll drop this knife and see where it lands. The second guy said, 'I'll drop this gun and see where it lands.' The third guy says, 'I'll drop this petrol bomb and see where it lands.' Then they all jump out of the plane and parachute down to see what the results are. The first guy sees this kid crying. He says, 'Hey, kid, why are you crying?' The kid explains that he has just got hit on the head by a knife. The second guy also finds a kid in tears and it turns out the kid got hit in the head by a gun. The third guy, however, finds a kid rolling on the ground laughing. 'Hey, kid,' he says. 'What's so funny?' The kid replies, 'I just farted and that building blew up!'

Her marriage into high society was an excuse for Lady Bountiful to entertain lavishly. Unfortunately, she was unused to all the rich food and soon found that she was permanently bloated and full of wind. Her embarrassment was complete when during a banquet for a visiting diplomat she let go a corker. So she blamed it on the butler who was standing behind her, crying loud enough for everyone in the room to hear, 'Jeeves, stop that!' To which Jeeves replied, 'Certainly, madam, which way did it go?'

Stepping into the elevator the businessman quickly detected an offensive odour. The only other occupant was a little old lady. 'Excuse me,' he addressed her, 'did you happen to break wind?' 'Of course I did,' she replied. 'You don't think I stink like this all the time, do you?'

Ab Mustafa was in the Arab bazaar one day when he felt a terrible pain in his stomach. He couldn't control the thunderous fart which followed. It boomed above the general hubbub and all around him were staggered. Ab Mustafa was so embarrassed that he ran home, packed his bags and left town. He didn't return for twenty years. Then, thinking it safe, he came back to find the bazaar much changed and modernized. At a carpet stall he asked a young boy who had built the new camel stables at the far end of the bazaar, and the young boy replied: 'Oh, that was built fourteen years and three days after Ab Mustafa farted in the bazaar and left town.'

A rather sad young man was still a virgin as he approached the ripe old age of thirty. So his mates lined him up with a willing and voracious young lady for his birthday present. Cheered on by his mates, the birthday boy had no choice but to go off with the woman. At first she stuck to basics but then she manoeuvred them into the soixante-neuf position. Unfortunately, she suddenly felt a rumble and let go a fart. The birthday boy got the full blast and threw her off him saying: 'Christ, what the hell is soixante-dix then?' Unfortunately for his mates, he is still a virgin.

A Red Indian chief has a problem passing wind so he sends son Number 1 to the doctor. The son arrives at the doctor's and says 'Big Chief No Fart'. The doctor gives son Number 1 some fart pills but he returns the next day and says 'Big Chief No Fart' and the following day 'Big Chief Still No Fart'. Eventually the doctor gives him the strongest laxatives he has in his possession and tells son Number 1 to give these to his father. The next day the doctor hears a wailing at the Indian camp and sets out to discover what is amiss. He sees son Number 1 being decked out in war paint and feathers. 'What news?' he asks him. The son replies, 'Big Fart No Chief'.

A guy walks into a bar and bets the bartender $20 that he can fart the national anthem. When the bartender agrees, the dude jumps up on the bar, squats, drops his pants and shits all over the bar...The bartender goes nuts and yells 'What the hell are you doing?' The farter explains, 'Hey, even Pavarotti has to clear his throat before a performance!'

What is the definition of a fart?
A turd honking for the right of way.

What do you get when you've been eating onions and beans?
Tear gas.

A man went into the doctor's and confessed to an embarrassing problem. 'I fart all the time, Doctor. But they are soundless and they are odourless. In fact, since I've been here, I've farted no less than five times. What do I do about it?' 'Here's a prescription, Mr Brown,' said the doctor. 'Take these pills three times daily for a week and then come back and see me.' The following week, a disappointed Mr Brown arrived at the surgery. 'Doctor, I'm farting as much as ever, but now they smell terrible as well.' 'Mr Brown,' said the doctor, 'think yourself a lucky man. Now that we've fixed your sinuses, we'll fix your hearing.'

What is green and smells?
Hulk's fart.

The Queen was showing the Archbishop of Canterbury around her new stables when a stallion near by let go such a resounding fart it rattled the windows and couldn't be ignored.

'Oh dear,' said the Queen, blushing, 'I'm frightfully sorry about that.'

'Think nothing of it, Ma'am,' said the archbishop. 'All actions are God-given. But anyway, I thought it was the stallion.'

In the geriatric ward, old Ben was dozing in his chair. Every time he leaned to one side a nurse would gently push him straight. A new patient arrived and asked how he found being in the ward: 'Oh it's all right,' said old Ben. 'But that young nurse makes it bloody difficult for one to have a fart.'

A girl really fancied a man. So when he asked her out for a date she was delighted. However, on the day of days she had a tummy bug. She couldn't bear to call the date off so she ate a lot of stomach-calming herbal tablets and waited for them to take effect. When he arrived, she dashed out of the flat giving him no time to come inside and smell the farty odour there. She got into his car and, as he waited for the traffic to ease up until he could open the driver's door, she thought she'd just risk letting a small one go. It was quite loud although thankfully not a stinker and she was just starting to relax when she heard a cough from behind her: 'Excuse me, dear, but may we introduce ourselves? We are John's parents.'

A fart: a belch that didn't find the lift.
A belch: a fart that caught the lift.

A wealthy playboy met a beautiful young girl in an exclusive lounge. He took her to his lavish apartment where he soon discovered she was not a tramp, but was well-groomed and very intelligent. Hoping to get her into bed he began to show her his collection of priceless antiques and paintings, and he offered her a glass of champagne. 'Oh I'd love a glass,' she replied. 'It is the most romantic, sexy drink on earth and just looking at an uncorked bottle fills me with the greatest excitement and anticipation. When the bubbles go up my nose, I am transported to a seventh heaven, and once I've finished the bottle I am so horny I am just about anybody's. On the other hand, I'll pass. All those bubbles make me fart.'

A woman who loved baked beans had to give them up because they caused her to fart too much. However, it was her birthday, and after having a few drinks at the office after work her resistance was lowered, so that she went into the fish-and-chip shop on the way home and ordered some pots of piping-hot baked beans. She figured that if she walked all the way home afterwards she could blow most of the effects out safely by the time she got there. Thus she set off at a brisk pace and soon began farting loudly.

Her husband met her at the door of her house, seeming worried that she was so much later than usual. 'Hurry up,' he said impatiently, 'I have a surprise for you.' Before he would let her over the threshold, he insisted that he blindfold her, and then he led her into the dining-room. 'Just wait here one minute,' he said, 'I'll be back in a tick.' As she sat waiting, she felt a burning sensation in her bottom and knew she had to let one go. So, taking advantage of the fact that her husband was out of the room, she parped away – at least five escaping in quick succession. Another minute passed and she farted a few more times until she heard her husband's footsteps returning. 'Happy birthday, darling,' he cried, removing her blindfold, and there sat six of her friends.

A guy comes home from the pub rolling drunk and falls into bed. His wife is asleep and he is glad that he hasn't woken her. He also feels free to let off a beer fart. The fart is loud and long and very, very smelly so that even its creator starts to choke. The wife also wakes up and says, 'What the hell was that?'

'Um . . . goal! One nil! GOAL!' replies the husband.

You drunk bastard, thinks the wife and squeezing her buttocks together tightly manages to fart herself. 'One all!' she snarls and rolls over and goes back to sleep.

You smug cow, thinks the husband, somewhat riled. He takes a few deep breaths, sucks in his stomach and . . . shits in the bed.

He reflects on his situation for a moment and then nudges his wife in the back: 'Oi, wake up. Half time, switch sides.'

Q: What's the definition of a surprise?
A: A fart with a lump in it.

A Japanese and an American are playing golf. The Japanese man gets ready to tee off but before he actually does so he sticks his thumb in front of his mouth and appears to be talking to it. The American says, 'What are you doing?' The Japanese replies, 'Oh, don't worry. I have a minute phone device inserted in my thumb and I was sending a message.' They continue to play golf and all of a sudden the American makes a noise that sounds like a fart. The Japanese looks over at him questioningly. 'Oh, says the American. Don't worry. I was just getting a message.'

An air-freshener seller gets into a lift where she is over-come by a rumbly tummy and lets go a shocker of a fart. 'Ah ha!' she thinks, 'no worries,' and takes out one of her samples of pine freshener and gives it a liberal spray.

At the next floor a man gets in. 'Christ,' he says, 'What's that smell?'

The lady replies: 'Oh, that's my pine air freshener.'

'Pine air freshener?' chokes the man. 'It smells more like someone shat on a Christmas tree.'

A guy is invited to dinner by his new girlfriend's parents. He is sitting at the table and their pet dog keeps biting at his ankles. He bends over to stop it and accidentally lets slip a fart. The girl's mother promptly cries, 'Rover, stop it, come away!' The guy is relieved and when another fart builds up, he just lets that one off too. 'Rover, PLEASE come away,' shouts the mother. The young man is now feeling safe enough to let go a third which rumbles loudly out of his backside. He looks at the dog accusingly and the girl's mother screams, 'Rover, come away now, before he shits on you.'

There was an old married couple who had lived together for nearly forty years. The only problem in their relationship was the husband's bad habit of breaking wind every morning – setting off his own dawn chorus. The wife was in despair and on their forty-first anniversary she awoke as usual with watering eyes and gasping for breath. Enough was enough, she decided. Up she got and went downstairs into the kitchen where she mixed together in a bowl mashed potatoes, gravy, uncooked liver, a haggis and red wine. Then she crept back upstairs with her bowl and, checking that her husband was indeed still asleep, and was indeed still farting away, she emptied the contents into the bed beside him.

An hour later she heard her husband wake up and then a couple of huge farts reverberate off the floorboards above her head. This was soon followed by a blood-curdling scream and the sound of frantic scurrying about upstairs. The wife could not control herself and burst out laughing, so much so that she had to put a tea-towel in her mouth to stop the guffaws. She had finally got her revenge.

Her husband appeared about half an hour later with the 'blood-stained' sheet and his pyjamas in his hand. He was very white and strangely quiet. He said 'Wife, you were right – all those years that I didn't listen to you and now I know I should have listened harder.'

'What do you mean?' asked the wife, trying to look innocent.

'Well you always told me that I would end up farting my guts out one of these days, and this morning it finally happened. But by the grace of God and these two fingers, I think I got them all back in.'

FARTING ALL OVER THE WORLD
Essential Farting Vocab.
For Travellers

When travelling around the world to farting conferences, I often find my specialized farting vocabulary indispensable. Here are some words and phrases for beer-drinking curry caters who find themselves adrift on foreign turf!

Language	Fartword	Fart rating as a nation
Afrikaans	poep	Strong gales 9/10
Albanian	mfryet	Weak breezes 2/10
Arabic	eegayas (with a big sound)	Moderate to good 7/10

Cantonese	fong	Blowy 6/10
Danish	fis	Strong gusts 8/10
Dutch	scheet	Gentle breezes 3/10
Finnish	pieru	Mediocre 5/10
French	pet	Force Ten expected 10/10
Gaelic	braim	Fair to middling 4/10
German	Furz	Thunderous 9/10
Greek	perdomai	Storms ahead 8/10

Hawaiian	pu'u puhi'u foully	Mild zephyrs 2/10
Hungarian	koz	Hot and dry winds 8/10
Italian	peto	Hot, dry winds 7/10
Japanese	hohi	Very low pressure 1/10
Latin	peditum	Poor 2/10
Norwegian	fis	Storm force 9/10
Polish	pierdzenic	Batten down the hatches 10/10
Portuguese	peido	Gentle breezes 6/10

Spanish	pedo	Southerly Force Eight 8/10
Swedish	fjärt	Gales expected 9/10
Thai	tod	Oriental winds 6/10
Welsh	gwynt	Fresh, light winds 5/10

WHEN IN FRANCE:

Où sont les toilettes? Je ne me sens pas bien.
Where is the toilet? I don't feel well.

Papier toilette
Toilet paper
(NB! Vital vocab. for all curry eaters)

Faut–il changer le combinaison pour le dîner?
Do I have to put on a new spacesuit for dinner?

Je n'arrive pas à ouvrir les fenêtres.
I can't get these windows open.

Ca sent pas la rose!
It smells. Or, literally, it doesn't smell like a rose.

WHEN IN SWEDEN:

Var vänlig visa mig till avdelningen för pruttkuddar.
Please point me to the whoopee-cushion department.

Er hund har visst fisit igen.
Your dog seems to have farted again.
(meaning 'Yes it was me, but I'd rather blame it on an innocent animal')

Är det mycket vitlök i den här grytan?
Does this stew contain a lot of garlic?

Man ska vädra sina åsikter.
One should give air to one's opinions.

WHEN IN SPAIN:

¡Quiero comer las judias por la cena!
I want to have beans for supper!

¡Me encanta el fiambre enlatado hecho con carne de cerdo!
I love Spam!

¿Donde esta los servicios?
Where is the loo?

No hay mas papel higiénico.
There is no loo paper left.

¿Tienes una máscara?
Do you have a mask?

¡Ten cuidado, mi perro va a eliminar gases!
Be careful, my dog is about to break wind.

WHEN IN SOUTH AFRICA:

Waar kan ek 'n kerrie ëet?
Where can I get a good curry?

Ek wil boentjies vir aandete he.
I want beans for supper.

Ek het te veel blomkool geëet.
I've eaten too much cabbage.

Dit luik sleg!
That smells terrible!

WHEN IN ITALY:

Questa birra tedesca mi fa scureggiare come una tromba!
This German beer is making me fart like a trumpet.

Lui ha appena fatto una puzza della Madonna!
He's just done a really smelly one!

Le tre scuregge (The 3 Farts):

1. Siquam: silenziosa quasi mortale – silent but
deadly/violent
2. Tadem: tanfo della madonna – a really smelly one
3. Bosef: boato senza fetore – a thunderer

Che puzza!
What a smell!

WHEN IN POLAND

Ten gulasz jest ostry!
This goulash is spicy!

Ta zupa z kapusty jest dobra.
This cabbage soup is good.

Chciaiabym jajko na smiadarnie.
I would like four eggs for breakfast.

To smierdzi okropnie w tym pokoju.
It smells bad in this room.

EVEN IN LATIN:

Estne ventilum hic?
Is there a fan in here?

Pullus fartus
Stuffed chicken

Licetne mihi in fabis pendere?
Can I pay in beans?

Facisne enemata?
Do you do enemas?

I need another operation on my rectum.
In recto meo aliam actionem chiurgi egeo.

Olface faeces meas; non valeo.
Smell my evacuations; I don't feel well.

Appendix

Alec Bromcie's favourite movies, songs, books, plays and poems

MOVIES:

Titanic
Chariots of Fire
Carry on Farting
Dirty Farting
Easy Farter
Farty Dancing
Flashfart
Fart and Fartability
My Best Friend's Fart
Muriel's Fart
How Green Was My Fart
Some Fart It Hot
Fart and Let Fart
Goldfarter
You Only Fart Twice
Farts are Forever
On Her Majesty's Secret Farts
Farts and Misdemeanours
White Men Can't Fart
The Postman Always Farts Twice

The Farters of Eastwick
The Empire Farts Back
Great Fart Expectations
Good Fart Hunting
Bravefart
Primary Farts
Fartless in Seattle
You Got Farts
Fartspotting.
Dead Farts' Society
Natural Fart Killers
Farts on a Train.
The Sound of Farts
Fart With the Wind
The Neverending Fart
Four Farts and a Funeral
Forrest Fart
Thunderbowel
Fartstock and One Smoking Barrel
The Ideal Fart

SONGS :

The Oscar-winning song, My Fart Will Go On
Blow the Wind Southerly
C'mon Baby, Light My Fart
Great Farts of Fire
Twist and Fart
FartaFartaFartaFartaFarta Chameleon
Fart Lightning
Fart From a Rose/Kiss From a Fart
Farty Woman
Wake Me Up Before You Fart-Fart
You're the Fart That I Want
Thank You For the Farts, For Giving Them To Me
Fart Around the Clock

Uptown Fart
Sea of Fart
Only Happy When It Farts
Say Phew, Say Me
The Wind Beneath My Jeans
La Bomba
Achy, Braky Fart
Boogie Bugle Butt of Company B
The Smells of Silence
Billy, Don't Eat a Hero
Killing Me Softly With His 'Song'
Breaking Wind Is Fun Toooo Do!
Oops, Strike a Match!
Fart Balls of Fire
You'll Never Fart Alone

LITERATURE:

The Farter in the Rye
Interview with the Fart
The Fart Song of J. Alfred Prufrock
A Midsummer Night's Fart
Much Afart About Nothing
Nineteen Eighty Fart
Brave New Fart
The Secret Fart of Adrian Mole
Fart of Darkness
To Kill a Fartingbird
Gone With the Wind
The Wind in the Willows
A High Wind in Jamaica
Whistle Down the Wind
A Breath of Fresh Air
Smell is Beautiful
The Farter Brown Stories
Fair Stood the Wind For France

BIBLIOGRAPHY & FURTHER READING

1) Tailwinds, Peter Furze, 1998; Michael O' Mara Books, London

2) *The Little Book of Farting*, Alec Bromcie, 1999; Michael O'Mara Books, London

3) *The History of Farting* (worldwide bestseller), Dr Benjamin Bart, 1995; Michael O'Mara Books, London

4) *Thunder, Flush & Thomas Crapper*, Adam Hart-Davis, 1997; Michael O'Mara Books, London

5) *The Little Toilet Book*, compiled by David Brown, 1999; Michael O'Mara Books, London

6) The next edition of this book

7) *Bubbles in the Bath* by Ivor Windybottom

8) Benjamin Franklin wrote a book called *Fart Proudly*. It is hard to find but you might be lucky enough to come across it.

PS! There are also many interesting fartsites on the Web these days for interested browsers.

★ Publisher's note: Unfortunately, *Fanny Farts – Myth or Just Damn Rude?* is currently out of print.

··

Alec Bromcie's Fartometer

Check your Recto-Scale rating!

Name: ....

Address:...

....

....

....Quantity..............

Mail to: Barking Spider Promotions, Trouser Cough Avenue, Guffton

160